THE 5 STAR ENTREPRENEUR

OWNING YOUR OWN

STUDY GUIDE

Copyright © 2021 by Dr. Chris Bowen

Published by Inspire

All rights reserved. No portion of this book may be reproduced, stored in a retrieval system, or transmitted in any form or by any means—electronic, mechanical, photocopy, recording, scanning, or other—except for brief quotations in critical reviews or articles, without prior written permission of the author.

Scripture quotations marked KJV are taken from the King James Version of the Bible. Public domain. Scripture quotations marked NIV are taken from the Holy Bible, New International Version®, NIV®. Copyright © 1973, 1978, 1984, 2011 by Biblica, Inc.™ Used by permission of Zondervan. All rights reserved worldwide. www.zondervan.com. The "NIV" and "New International Version" are trademarks registered in the United States Patent and Trademark Office by Biblica, Inc.™ | Scripture quotations marked NKJV are taken from the New King James Version®. Copyright © 1982 by Thomas Nelson. Used by permission. All rights reserved. | Scripture quotations marked TLB are taken from The Living Bible copy- right © 1971 by Tyndale House Foundation. Used by permission of Tyndale House Publishers Inc., Carol Stream, Illinois 60188. All rights reserved. The Living Bible, TLB, and The Living Bible logo are registered trademarks of Tyndale House Publishers. | Scripture quotations marked NLT are taken from the *Holy Bible*, New Living Translation, copyright © 1996, 2004, 2015 by Tyndale House Foundation. Used by permission of Tyndale House Publishers, Inc., Carol Stream, Illinois 60188. All rights reserved. | Scripture quotations marked MSG are taken from *THE MESSAGE*, copyright © 1993, 1994, 1995, 1996, 2000, 2001, 2002 by Eugene H. Peterson. Used by permission of NavPress. All rights reserved. Represented by Tyndale House Publishers, Inc. | Scripture quotations marked GNT are from the Good News Translation in Today's English Version—Second Edition. Copyright © 1992 by American Bible Society. Used by Permission.

For foreign and subsidiary rights, contact the author.

Cover design by: Joe De Leon
Author photo on cover: Andrew van Tilborgh

ISBN: 978-1-954089-66-2   1 2 3 4 5 6 7 8 9 10

Printed in the United States of America

THE 5 STAR ENTREPRENEUR

OWNING YOUR OWN

DR. CHRISTOPHER BOWEN

STUDY GUIDE

CONTENTS

Chapter 1. Why Financial Freedom? 6

Chapter 2. What is Financial Freedom? 12

Chapter 3. Say Yes to No Debt 18

Chapter 4. Practical Principles for Savings 24

Chapter 5. Proven Prosperity Principles 30

Chapter 6. Reasonable Debt Reduction 36

Chapter 7. Five Keys to Building Multiple
           Streams of Income 42

Chapter 8. Why Entrepreneurship? 48

Chapter 9. Enjoying Your Financial Freedom 54

chapter 1

WHY FINANCIAL FREEDOM?

Being financially free, financially prosperous, simply means having control over your life. When you have control over your life, your finances will line up accordingly.

Reading Time

As you read Chapter 1: "Why Financial Freedom?" in *The 5-Star Entrepreneur*, review, reflect on, and respond to the text by answering the following questions.

REVIEW, REFLECT, AND RESPOND:

What does prosperity look like for your life? What does being prosperous mean to you?

_____
_____
_____
_____
_____
_____
_____
_____
_____
_____
_____

What is one thing you want to be financially free from?

_____
_____
_____
_____
_____
_____
_____
_____
_____
_____
_____

> **Reflect on**
>
> *Let no debt remain outstanding, except the continuing debt to love one another, for whoever loves others has fulfilled the law.*
>
> *—Romans 13:8 (NIV)*

Consider Romans 13:8 and answer the following questions:

The debt to love one another is a debt that can't be repaid. Have you ever neglected that obligation in any relationship?

_____
_____
_____
_____

Who is "one another"? Who is Paul calling us to love?

_____
_____
_____
_____

How can you apply this verse to your finances?

_____
_____
_____
_____

In what area(s) do you overspend? How can you take steps to reduce spending money in that area?

_____
_____
_____
_____
_____
_____

If you tracked every penny you spent, what would you learn about your spending habits?

_____
_____
_____
_____
_____
_____

If money and education weren't factors, what would you be doing? Can you do that on your current budget? If not, what steps can you take to start planning out how to reach that goal?

_____
_____
_____
_____
_____
_____

How would you encourage someone who is struggling to limit their recreational spending?

Write about a time when you heeded God's instructions and prospered because of it.

What would you do to double $1,000 in one year? How would you continue to double your profit for the next ten years to become a millionaire?

Why is thinking outside the box necessary to becoming a 5 Star Entrepreneur?

_____
_____
_____
_____
_____
_____
_____

What is the biggest financial takeaway you learned from Chapter 1?

_____
_____
_____
_____
_____
_____

chapter 2

WHAT IS FINANCIAL FREEDOM?

You have to decide, "My financial future is up to me." Nobody else can determine it for you.

Reading Time

As you read Chapter 2: "What is Financial Freedom?" in *The 5-Star Entrepreneur*, review, reflect on, and respond to the text by answering the following questions.

REVIEW, REFLECT, AND RESPOND:

Financial freedom means different things to different people. What does financial freedom mean to you?

_____
_____
_____
_____
_____
_____
_____
_____

How much money would you require to have saved up to consider yourself financially free?

_____
_____
_____
_____
_____
_____
_____
_____

> **Reflect on**
>
> *A good person leaves an inheritance for their children's children, but a sinner's wealth is stored up for the righteous.*
>
> —*Proverbs 13:22 (NIV)*

Consider Proverbs 13:22 and answer the following questions:

How can you work toward leaving an inheritance for your future generations?

_____
_____
_____
_____
_____

What does this verse say about the value of leaving an inheritance?

_____
_____
_____
_____
_____

How can you apply this verse to your finances?

_____
_____
_____
_____
_____

Why that number?

_____
_____
_____
_____

Why is it important to take responsibility of your financial situation?

_____
_____
_____
_____

Make a list of three charities or causes to whom you'd be interested in giving. Note the percent you'd be able to feasibly contribute.

1. _____
2. _____
3. _____

Do you have any spending "addictions"? How could you mitigate those?

_____
_____
_____
_____

On a scale of one to ten, how disciplined are you generally? How does this contribute to your financial situation?

_____
_____
_____

In what area within the financial realm are you the weakest? Be brutally honest and evaluate where you're at.

_____
_____
_____
_____
_____

What temptations should you get rid of to avoid unnecessary spending?

_____
_____
_____
_____
_____

Review the six income stream examples that Chris shares. Which of those piques your interest the most? Why?

_____
_____
_____
_____
_____

What is the biggest financial takeaway you learned from Chapter 2?

_____
_____
_____

chapter 3

SAY YES TO NO DEBT

In order to say yes to no debt, you first have to say no to instant self-gratification.

Reading Time

As you read Chapter 3: "Say Yes to No Debt" in *The 5-Star Entrepreneur*, review, reflect on, and respond to the text by answering the following questions.

REVIEW, REFLECT, AND RESPOND:

How can we combat our temptation to succumb to instant gratification?

_____
_____
_____
_____
_____
_____
_____
_____
_____
_____

Who is someone in your life that will hold you financially accountable?

_____
_____
_____
_____
_____
_____
_____
_____

Reflect on

Whoever gives heed to instruction prospers, and blessed is the one who trusts in the Lord

—Proverbs 16:20 (NIV)

Consider Proverbs 16:20 and answer the following questions:

Write about a time you prospered because you followed instructions.

___

Have you ever experienced negative consequences after following instructions? What did you take away from that?

___

How can you apply this verse to your finances?

___

Make a list of your top three debts and the interest percent you pay for each. Do any interest rates surprise you?

1. _____

2. _____

3. _____

From your list of debts, which one will you target first to eliminate? What steps will you take to do so?

_____
_____
_____
_____
_____
_____
_____

Have you known someone who spent money without thinking or to flaunt their status? How did their financial situation pan out later?

_____
_____
_____
_____
_____
_____
_____

What can you replace retail therapy with if you struggle with shopping to make yourself feel better?

_____
_____
_____
_____
_____
_____
_____

What is one way you can financially prepare for and endure crisis?

_____
_____
_____
_____
_____
_____
_____

What is challenging about making a budget? How can you overcome that obstacle?

___

What steps can you proactively take moving forward to say yes to no debt?

___

What is the biggest financial takeaway you learned from Chapter 3?

___

chapter 4

PRACTICAL PRINCIPLES FOR SAVINGS

Wealth should be obtained not so that we can have things, but so that we can fund ministry, help others, and live comfortably for the rest of our lives.

Reading Time

As you read Chapter 4: "Practical Principles for Savings" in *The 5-Star Entrepreneur*, review, reflect on, and respond to the text by answering the following questions.

REVIEW, REFLECT, AND RESPOND:

What is your ideal retirement age? What practices are you putting in place to have a healthy amount of savings when you reach that age?

_____
_____
_____
_____
_____
_____
_____
_____
_____

Which mindset do you feed more—being rich or being poor? How does it affect your daily financial habits?

_____
_____
_____
_____
_____
_____
_____
_____

> **Reflect on**
>
> *The wise have wealth and luxury, but fools spend whatever they get.*
>
> *—Proverbs 21:20 (NLT)*

Consider Proverbs 21:20 and answer the following questions:

How would you encourage someone who spends whatever they get to start saving?

_____
_____
_____
_____
_____

Why is it foolish to spend whatever you get?

_____
_____
_____
_____
_____

How can you apply this verse to your finances?

_____
_____
_____
_____
_____

Do you have six months' worth of expenses saved up? If not, how can you cut costs to get there?

_____
_____
_____
_____
_____

Have you ever caught yourself giving one of the four excuses Chris states for why you don't save? Which one are you most likely to fall victim to believing and why?

_____
_____
_____
_____
_____

What is your biggest barrier in starting right now to save money?

_____
_____
_____
_____
_____

Why is being patient important to reaching your financial goals?

_____
_____
_____
_____
_____

What is really important to you? How will being financially free help foster what matters in your life?

_____
_____
_____
_____
_____

In what ways can you "commit to being rich"? What ideas can you capitalize on to "think big" in order to become wealthy?

_____
_____
_____
_____
_____

Do you practice any of the seven techniques Chris gives to save money? Which of those can you implement into your daily life and practices?

_____
_____
_____
_____
_____

What is the biggest financial takeaway you learned from Chapter 4?

_____
_____
_____
_____

chapter 5

PROVEN PROSPERITY PRINCIPLES

There are no get-rich-quick schemes to follow that will result in true, lasting wealth.

Reading Time

As you read Chapter 5: "Proven Prosperity Principles" in *The 5-Star Entrepreneur*, review, reflect on, and respond to the text by answering the following questions.

REVIEW, REFLECT, AND RESPOND:

How can you operate in faith with your money to move God's hand on your finances?

_____
_____
_____
_____
_____
_____
_____
_____
_____
_____

Chris says, "The more we give, the more God can bless us." What ways are you giving? In what ways would you like to start giving?

_____
_____
_____
_____
_____
_____
_____
_____
_____
_____

> **Reflect on**
>
> *Give, and you will receive. Your gift will return to you in full—pressed down, shaken together to make room for more, running over, and poured into your lap. The amount you give will determine the amount you get back.*
>
> *—Luke 6:38 (NLT)*

Consider Luke 6:38 and answer the following questions:

Are you giving just for the sake of receiving? Why or why not?

_____
_____
_____
_____

What do you think we receive when we give? Could Luke mean something other than receiving money?

_____
_____
_____
_____

How can you apply this verse to your finances?

_____
_____
_____
_____

Do you know someone who tries to control how their giving is handled? Do you agree or disagree with how they give

Are you guilty of wasting time worrying about money, bills, or making ends meet? What can you do to better manage your time?

What kind of spending patterns are you perpetuating that aren't healthy for your finances?

In what ways do you compare what you have with what others have?

_____
_____
_____
_____
_____
_____
_____
_____

What things can you learn to live without?

_____
_____
_____
_____
_____
_____
_____
_____

Do you operate by a written budget? Why or why not?

___

What financial area do you want to grow in? Who can you seek out who has wisdom in that area?

___

What is the biggest financial takeaway you learned from Chapter 5?

chapter 6

REASONABLE DEBT REDUCTION

The only debt God commissions us to look at is the debt we have to love each other.

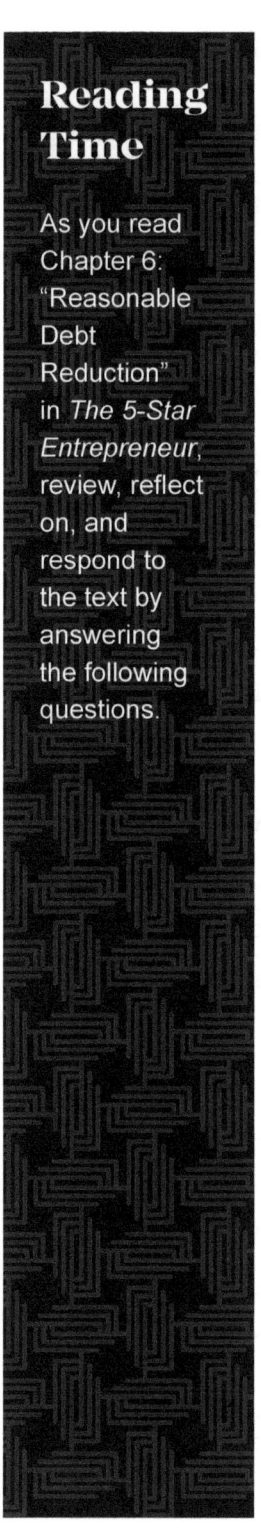

Reading Time

As you read Chapter 6: "Reasonable Debt Reduction" in *The 5-Star Entrepreneur*, review, reflect on, and respond to the text by answering the following questions.

REVIEW, REFLECT, AND RESPOND:

In what ways can you be patient while paying off debts and gathering wealth?

_____
_____
_____
_____
_____
_____
_____
_____
_____

Which financial class would you categorize yourself in: lower, middle, or upper? Does it matter to you what class you're in? Why or why not?

_____
_____
_____
_____
_____
_____
_____
_____

Reflect on

But seek first his kingdom and his righteousness, and all these things will be given to you as well.

—Matthew 6:33 (NIV)

Consider Matthew 6:33 and answer the following questions:

How do you know if you're truly seeking God's Kingdom first?

_____
_____
_____
_____

How do worries and anxieties manifest in our lives when we don't seek God first?

_____
_____
_____
_____

How can you apply this verse to your finances?

_____
_____
_____
_____

Are you in control of your money, or is your money in control of you? What can you do to put yourself in control of your money?

_____
_____
_____
_____

Is your soul prosperous through faith and prayer? How can that transfer over to financial prosperity?

_____
_____
_____
_____

Are you guilty of spending your health to obtain wealth? Why is that a bad thing?

_____
_____
_____
_____

What specific steps can you take to lower your credit score?

_____
_____
_____
_____

Are you a good steward of what God has given to you? Why or why not?

_____

_____

_____

_____

_____

Which of the ten principles for debt reduction are you most likely to implement? Why?

_____

_____

_____

_____

_____

Do you possess the three qualities it takes to get out of debt? Which do you struggle with the most?

_____

_____

_____

_____

_____

What is the biggest financial takeaway you learned from Chapter 6?

_____

_____

_____

_____

_____

chapter 7

FIVE KEYS TO BUILDING MULTIPLE STREAMS OF INCOME

Everybody is unique, and everybody is going to build wealth differently.

Reading Time

As you read Chapter 7: "Five Keys to Building Multiple Streams of Income" in *The 5-Star Entrepreneur*, review, reflect on, and respond to the text by answering the following questions.

REVIEW, REFLECT, AND RESPOND:

Why is it important to have a healthy attitude for saving money and building wealth?

_____
_____
_____
_____
_____
_____
_____
_____
_____
_____

Which letter of the WEALTH acronym do you struggle with the most? Why?

_____
_____
_____
_____
_____
_____
_____
_____
_____
_____

Reflect on

My people are destroyed from lack of knowledge.

—Hosea 4:6a (NIV)

Consider Hosea 4:6a and answer the following questions:

Why is the lack of knowledge about God so dangerous?

_____
_____
_____
_____
_____

How do we gain knowledge about God and how does it affect our walk with Him?

_____
_____
_____
_____
_____
_____

How can you apply this verse to your finances?

_____
_____
_____
_____
_____

What is one financial habit you want to be more consistent in?

_____
_____
_____
_____

Are you focused on your finances? What can you do to increase your focus?

_____
_____
_____
_____

What is one of the biggest distractions from your finances you face in your life?

_____
_____
_____
_____

Are you fully leveraging your gifts or talents? If not, how could you start?

_____
_____
_____
_____

How can you go about gaining more knowledge in your particular market or industry?

_____
_____
_____
_____
_____

What is your "niche"? What are you good at, and how can you monetize that?

_____
_____
_____
_____
_____
_____
_____

Which of the five financial habits outlined by Chris do you struggle with the most? How can you change that?

_____
_____
_____
_____
_____
_____
_____

What is the biggest financial takeaway you learned from Chapter 7?

_____
_____
_____
_____
_____
_____
_____

chapter 8

WHY ENTREPRENEURSHIP?

Wealth was never designed just to give you a bigger house or more expensive toys. It was designed to give you freedom.

Reading Time

As you read Chapter 8: "Why Entrepreneurship?" in *The 5-Star Entrepreneur*, review, reflect on, and respond to the text by answering the following questions.

REVIEW, REFLECT, AND RESPOND:

What is one of the biggest worries you have about becoming an entrepreneur? How can you work to overcome it?

_____
_____
_____
_____
_____
_____
_____
_____
_____

What are your core values or non-negotiables?

_____
_____
_____
_____
_____
_____
_____
_____
_____

Reflect on

Honor the Lord with your wealth, with the firstfruits of all your crops; then your barns will be filled to overflowing, and your vats will brim over with new wine.

—Proverbs 3:9-10 (NIV)

Consider Proverbs 3:9-10 and answer the following questions:

What is one glorifying way to honor God with your wealth?

_____
_____
_____
_____
_____

What are the implications of honoring the Lord with your wealth?

_____
_____
_____
_____
_____

How can you apply this verse to your finances?

_____
_____
_____
_____
_____

What business, fueled by your passions, would you be able to start that would require low overhead costs to get started?

_____
_____
_____
_____

What aspect about being your own boss is the most appealing to you?

_____
_____
_____
_____

How will your entrepreneurial business make a difference in someone's life?

_____
_____
_____
_____

What are you willing to change in your life in order to make it better?

_____
_____
_____
_____

Do you believe you have what it takes to be a business leader? In what area could you improve?

_____
_____
_____
_____

What makes you excited? How can you capitalize on that to become a successful entrepreneur?

_____
_____
_____
_____

Which of the seven benefits of being a 5-Star Entrepreneur sounds the most appealing to you? Why?

_____
_____
_____
_____

What is the biggest financial takeaway you learned from Chapter 8?

_____
_____
_____
_____

chapter 9

ENJOYING YOUR FINANCIAL FREEDOM

Whatever the situation you find yourself in today financially, it's not too late to turn around and get back on the right road.

Reading Time

As you read Chapter 9: "Enjoying Your Financial Freedom" in *The 5-Star Entrepreneur*, review, reflect on, and respond to the text by answering the following questions.

REVIEW, REFLECT, AND RESPOND:

Staying financially free requires four traits: determination, discipline, decisions, and direction. Which of these do you find the most difficult to uphold?

_____
_____
_____
_____
_____
_____
_____
_____

List the first two steps you'll take to live your life on purpose and become financially free.

1. _____
_____
_____
_____

2. _____
_____
_____
_____

Reflect on

The beginning of wisdom is this: Get wisdom.
Though it cost all you have, get understanding.

—Proverbs 4:7 (NIV)

Consider Proverbs 4:7 and answer the following questions:

Why does gaining understanding cost all you have? What does that say about the importance of wisdom?

_____
_____
_____
_____
_____

In what way does biblical wisdom apply to your finances?

_____
_____
_____
_____
_____

How can you apply this verse to your finances?

_____
_____
_____
_____
_____

How are you stewarding what God has given to you? What ways could you improve your stewardship?

_____
_____
_____
_____
_____
_____
_____

What good financial habits should you start practicing in order to undo the habits that have caused you to become financially bound?

_____
_____
_____
_____
_____
_____

Is there any aspect of your life that is making you financially stagnant?

_____
_____
_____
_____
_____
_____
_____

Which type of discipline resonates the most with you: preventative, supportive, or corrective? Why?

_____
_____
_____
_____
_____
_____

How will you make financial decisions differently in post-pandemic times compared to pre-pandemic times?

_____
_____
_____
_____
_____
_____

Out of the four problems Chris lists that can prevent effective decision-making, which one do you find yourself most closely tied with? How can you resolve it?

_____
_____
_____
_____
_____
_____

Do you have clear direction for your financial journey? How can you use the four tips Chris gives to have clear direction?

_____
_____
_____
_____
_____
_____

Are you ready to start your financial journey? List the first step you'll take as a takeaway from this book.

_____
_____
_____
_____
_____
_____